THE TEACHER'S SAINT

SAINT JOHN BAPTIST DE LA SALLE
PATRON SAINT OF TEACHERS

George Van Grieken, FSC

Interior design and composition by Laurie Nelson, Agapé Design Studios (agapedesignstudios.com).

Cover design by River Design.

Production and distribution by Saint Mary's Press (www.smp.org).

Back cover quotation: De La Salle, John Baptist, *Meditations by St. John Baptist de La Salle*, trans. Richard Arnandez, and Augustine Loes, eds. Augustine Loes and Francis Huether, (Landover, MD: Christian Brothers Conference, 1994), 256 (Meditation 139.3).

Front cover photo: A 1901 painting by Giovanni Gagliardi (1860-1908). John Baptist de La Salle shows a classroom to the pastor of the parish of Saint Sulpice, the location of the first Lasallian school in Paris.

Back cover photo: A portrait of John Baptist de La Salle painted by Pierre Léger in 1734. It has been adopted as the official portrait of the Founder and is a reminder of the description left by a biographer who lived with him: "His face was always happy, tranquil, and imperturbable... The image of kindness that characterized him also produced a joy among those around him" (Blain, Book 4, p. 308).

Interior Images: All images, paintings, sketches, or graphics inside this book have come either from publications by the Institute of the Brothers of the Christian Schools or from publicly accessible, non-copyrighted sources such as Wikipedia Commons.

Printed in the United States of America

978-1-884904-16-5

TABLE OF CONTENTS

A 1901 painting by Giovanni Gagliardi (1860-1908). John Baptist de La Salle shows a classroom to the pastor of the parish of San Sulpice, the location of the first Lasallian school in Paris.

INTRODUCTION

Saint John Baptist de La Salle was born in 1651, lived a life that he had never anticipated, and passed into eternal life on April 7, 1719, in Rouen, France. Canonized in 1900, he was declared the Patron Saint of All Teachers of Youth on May 15, 1950. This short book fills in some of the details of his remarkable life.

Here was someone who founded a new way of teaching and a unique set of Catholic schools, called the "Christian Schools" in his time. Run by a group of men who were called the Brothers of the Christian Schools, they became today's Institute of the Brothers of the Christian Schools (De La Salle Christian Brothers), with its mission "to provide a human and Christian education to the young, especially the poor, according to the ministry which the Church has entrusted to it." (*Rule,* art.3)

It was De La Salle's persistent, faith-filled, and zealous pursuit of where God was leading him that resulted in the worldwide educational movement that is still growing every year, animated by Brothers—the consecrated religious men who dedicate their lives to this same mission—and many other educators who are inspired by Saint John Baptist de La Salle's charism.

There is something in his story, in his writings, and in his living spirit that plants itself in the hearts of teachers everywhere. From whatever background and from whatever culture, they find themselves drawn to an educational vision and approach that reminds them of why they became involved in teaching in the first place. Here is a person and a charism worth knowing, especially for those involved in education. Here is a remarkable individual who continues to shape the educational world of today in ways he could not have imagined, inspiring educators of all kinds, shaping how they see students, teachers, and the activity of teaching. His writings, insights, and example wonderfully and naturally resonate with the experience of educators everywhere.

John Baptist de La Salle is someone who is a true saint for all teachers.

— *George Van Grieken, FSC*

IN HIS OWN WORDS

John Baptist de La Salle never wanted to start a religious order, let alone an educational movement that would have him declared as the patron saint of all teachers of youth in 1950 by Pope Pius XII, or that would in 2019 have 4,000 Brothers and 90,000 Lasallian Partners teaching 1,000,000 pupils in more than 1,000 establishments in 80 countries of the world. All he wanted to do as a young man was to become a good priest working for the Church in 17th-century France. Yet one thing led to another, and before he realized it he was involved with a group of rather slovenly men of marginal intelligence running a couple of gratuitous, parish-based, inner-city schools for streetwise 10- to 14-year-old boys whose expertise in gambling,

Image: (above) A portrait of John Baptist de La Salle painted by Pierre Léger in 1734. It has been adopted as the official portrait of the Founder and is a reminder of the description left by a biographer who lived with him: "His face was always happy, tranquil, and imperturbable... The image of kindness that characterized him also produced a joy among those around him" (Blain, Book 4, p. 308).

rough-housing, and petty vice overshadowed any thought of reading, writing, and Christian responsibility. He writes much later on:

> *I had imagined that the care which I assumed of the schools and the masters would amount only to a marginal involvement committing me to no more than providing for the subsistence of the masters and assuring that they acquitted themselves of their tasks with piety and devotedness.... If I had ever thought that the care I was taking of the schoolmasters out of pure charity would ever have made it my duty to live with them, I would have dropped the whole project.... Indeed, I experienced a great deal of unpleasantness when I first had them come to my house. This lasted two years. It was undoubtedly for this reason that God, who guides all things with wisdom and serenity, whose way it is not to force the inclinations of persons, willed to commit me entirely to the development of the schools. He did this in an imperceptible way and over a long period of time so that one commitment led to another in a way that I did not foresee in the beginning.[1]*

So how did this all come about? We won't go into all of the fascinating details, but the highlights can be presented easily enough. For those interested in a more complete picture of the life of De La Salle, there are resources recommended at the end of this little book that provide an opportunity to develop a deeper appreciation of his history, character, and writings.

A 1701 painting of King Louis XIV of France (1643 – 1715) in his coronation robes, painted by Rigaud Condé Chantilly (1659-1743).

De La Salle's World

De La Salle grew up in a world without electricity, cars, TV, radio, phones, texts, computer, or internet. He couldn't simply flick a switch to have light, couldn't go fairly quickly almost anywhere he wanted to go, couldn't check his facts on the smartphone, and couldn't communicate instantly with almost anyone in the world. His was a world of candlelight, horse carriages, walking, libraries, letter-writing, conversations and house visits, frequent illness or death, and firm social classes and cultural limitations.

Social and Economic Context

This was the age of King Louis XIV, the "Sun King" who ruled France with an iron—if clever—fist. It was an age when social standing, good manners, benefices, political intrigue, and grand living were the rule. And that was just in the Church! The State had all of this plus it was engaged in one war after another, taxed the population as much as it could tolerate, followed a system of governance and justice that had as many exceptions as it had applications, and for a time built up France's status to that of a "superpower." Along the way, the poor remained quite poor and many of the rich became even richer, although a good number of the more industrious artisans, shopkeepers, and minor officials managed to have an increasingly influential voice in public affairs.

Economically, Europe was a mixed bag of "haves" and "have-nots," with certain countries or areas within a country enjoying prosperity while other areas languished. Customs duties had to be paid at each town or province through which products passed. As a result, smuggling was an accepted way of life. European economies, being based largely on agriculture, experienced frequent crises, especially if a particular year's crops failed. When these crises happened, starvation and widespread epidemics were sure to follow.

Two-thirds of the over 20 million French people lived in the countryside in small villages of two or three hundred. These villages provided the agricultural base on which the country stood. One-fifth of France's land was occupied by small farms that supported the rest of the population. People in both the countryside and the towns rose at dawn and retired at sunset. Six or seven day workweeks were the norm, with each workday lasting up to 14 hours. The French daily diet for most people consisted mainly of coarse bread, cheese, and some meat for their one cooked meal a day. For vegetables, there were onions that would be added to thicken a simple grain stew, various locally grown vegetables if you could afford it, and herbs that garnished the rare beef, mutton, pork, rabbit, fish, or fowl. Drinkable water was scarce and iffy. The beverages of choice for the majority were watered down wine, cider, and weak beer.

In towns, the guilds *(corps de métiers)* were powerful fraternities of tradespeople such as butchers, barrel makers, carpenters, masons, writing masters, and others. They might be considered similar to the professional or trade organizations of today, although their advocacy posture bears more resemblance to that of today's unions. Each guild had regulations that governed its particular trade, specifying the number of shops, apprentices, clerks, and other details. This also applied to those providing education. Such guilds both ensured common standards, such as they were, and safeguarded an effective monopoly.

After the sporadic economic efforts of earlier Ministers of Finance, many of whom succeeded primarily in accumulating vast amounts of personal wealth, Louis XIV's finance minister, Jean-Baptiste Colbert (1641-1683), initiated and subsidized basic and essential industries and soon turned France's economy around, increasing the government's wealth substantially. But deficit spending as a result of the Dutch War (1672-1679) caused his plans to unravel, and France's financial difficulties again dominated the economic scene. It was primarily this economic downturn that provided the backdrop for De La Salle's initial educational endeavors.

Taxation was a main source of income for the various governing bodies, but its collection was neither consistent nor fair. One author writes that the tax system in France at that time "would seem to have been designed with the sole object of ensuring a minimum return to the king at a maximum price to his subjects, with the heaviest share falling on the poorest section of the population."[2] Who paid taxes and how much each one paid was based more on one's social class than on anything else. The peasants, urban poor, and lower classes were burdened with the bulk of the government's taxation. At every emergency, the main direct tax, called the *taille,* was increased. Its only limit was "the government's estimate of what a province could bear without revolt..."[3] The hardship of taxation had led to what came to be called the *Fronde* riots in Paris (1648-1653), which unsuccessfully tried to limit the encroaching reach of the king into people's lives and pockets. Taxation would remain a very volatile issue among the French people.

On the social scene, after 1680 and the rise of Colbert from the bourgeoisie—the middle class of the time—to the state's highest offices, birth no longer was the only measure of a person's worth in France. Merchants, wealthy artisans, bishops, and city council members all jostled for positions of influence. The upper bourgeoisie, which included the De La Salle family, consisted of nobles, royal officials, the medical and legal professions, and the wealthiest master-craftsmen. These lived a fairly comfortable lifestyle. The artisan class of the time was part of the "petite bourgeoisie."

These were the independent master-craftsmen, the small traders, and the shopkeepers who were able to weather difficult times, remaining relatively well-off but having no voice in the running of the town's affairs.

The Poor

The poor of the 17th century were in a vastly different situation from that of the poor in today's Western culture. Today's standard considers as "poor" all those who cannot afford the minimal comforts enjoyed by the lowest wage-earner. Such a standard would include most people of 17th-century France. The standard of that time, however, considered as "poor" all those who had neither steady income nor savings for times of unemployment; that is, no real security for surviving an economic crisis. The "destitute," moreover, were in a social category encompassing all those whose insecurity was a continual way of life. The destitute rarely ate enough or survived winters without a reliable source of heat, and they didn't get married until they were able to afford a family, usually after the age of 30. Both the "poor" and the "destitute" were at the mercy of the seasons and harvest, regularly experiencing periods of unemployment and semi-starvation.

The poor did have a few charitable resources at their disposal. Each parish had an official register of those who were poor and who lived within its boundaries, and the parish would accept gifts or money for them. Monasteries regularly distributed bread and soup, providing shelter to wandering beggars. A poor tax was levied on all non-indigent citizens for the purpose of sustaining the poor. Judicial magistrates, instead of sending wealthy individuals to prison, might impose heavy fines on them, directing such funds to various agencies for the benefit of the poor. All school teachers were to accept poor children without charge, although the limited clothing, language, and hygiene of the poor (not to mention the minimal costs involved in purchasing school supplies) kept almost all of them away. In the general scheme of 17th-century French society, the poor and destitute occupied a position of dependence and inferiority that is difficult to appreciate fully today.

Wherever I go I will find you, my God; there is no place that is not honored by your presence.

— *Explanation of the Method of Interior Prayer*

Religious Context

Religiously, France in the 17th century was a country wherein the Church and the State were intimately linked together. The Catholic Church owned one-fourth to one-third of the national wealth. From the time of the 5th century and the decline of the Roman Empire's influence in France, the Church had increasingly exercised its strong administrative structure within the country. As the first of the three *estates*, or classes, into which the kingdom was divided (clergy, nobility, and commoners), the Church enjoyed great prestige. Along with its status, however, the Church performed many important and vital social functions. All works of charity, including education, were under the Church's control. Clergy and religious built the buildings, provided the personnel, and often financially underwrote the schools, poor houses, and hospitals that provided what we might call social services today.

From the king down, the Church's involvement was wide and deep. King Louis XIV considered himself a devout Catholic and strove to remain as such. He made proposals regarding religious matters to clerical assemblies and requested their financial and moral support in social and economic schemes. He selected bishops by sending the pope a list of favorites. Church officials presided together with lay magistrates in the supreme law courts. Police routinely enforced fasting and abstinence during Lent, arresting butchers, for example, who were open on Fridays. Every organization and religious community needed *letters patent* from the king (similar to today's Articles of Incorporation) in order to have legal status. People looked to the parish as the country's basic religious and administrative center. Every village was first of all a parish, and the priest was second in rank behind the local nobleman. It was through the parish that most French people encountered the substance of their government.

Church life was intense and extensive. Saint Sulpice in Paris had its first Mass at 4:00 a.m. every day, with many people in attendance. Twenty-five Masses a day would not be uncommon. Daily Mass was also part of the normal routine in parish charity schools, as it came to be in De La Salle's "Christian Schools," a name that at the time would have the import of what "Catholic School" conveys today.

If you cannot pray, tell God that you cannot and then remain at peace. He will not ask you to do the impossible. Or, say to him as the Apostles did, "Lord, teach me to pray." Then remain humbly before him as one who is incapable of doing anything, and that will be your prayer.

— *Letter 111*

French Spirituality

In French spirituality, growing interest in contemplation and mysticism was joined with the Catholic affirmation of uniting faith with action that emerged from the Counter-Reformation and the Council of Trent (1545-1563). The ideal of personal renewal through religious devotion and works of mercy started by Italy's *Oratory of Divine Love* (1497) was quickly followed by other religious groups dedicated to the reform of the clergy and to doing good works. The "French School of Spirituality," associated with Cardinal de Bérulle (1575-1629), greatly influenced De La Salle's early seminary training, and this is evident in De La Salle's writings.

This French School of Spirituality stressed the necessity of one's personal *kenosis* (self-emptying) in order to be filled with Christ. The Christian made explicit acts of faith in the "principal Christian mysteries" (the Trinity, the Incarnation, the Redemption, and so on), incarnating the very being of Jesus by adopting actions and interior attitudes similar to those Christ first brought to reality by His every deed, His every feeling, His every outlook—in terms used by the French School, His every "mystery" and "disposition." By entering into Christ's sentiments and dispositions, one entered into Christ's mystical reality of salvation and thereby came to act, and to be, more and more like Him.

This was also a time when Jansenism's serious and rigorous outlook on the economy of grace working within what they saw as an essentially corrupt human nature, led to a rather negative view of the possibility of salvation. By making original sin and the absolute, constant need of grace the focal point of Christian belief, the idea of an uphill battle in pursuit of salvation came to the fore. At the same time, Quietism, a radical stance of inactivity, arose through a distrust of human initiative in the economy of grace, preaching passivity of soul, particularly with regard to prayer. And Gallicanism insisted on the independence of the French bishops from Rome, denying the personal infallibility of the pope, and severely limiting papal authority over temporal rulers.

While he was greatly influenced by the French spirituality and the various ideological movements of his time, De La Salle "uniquely blended a number of dimensions present in the French School into his new community: the apostolate, the importance of education, a sense of the needy, the element of service, and so on. As the French School, among its male representatives, had stressed the priesthood as the experienced example of commitment to Jesus, so now La Salle stressed the apostolate of teaching as an expression of [discipleship to] Jesus."[4]

Simply put, De La Salle applied to primary school teaching and lay teachers what the ideological momentum of the Council of Trent had applied to seminary teaching and priests.

Educational Context

On the educational front, before and during the time of King Louis XIV, education was discussed as heatedly as theology and politics. France had a well-established school system geared almost exclusively to the non-poor, consisting of schools, colleges, and universities run by religious orders, secular priests, and lay professors. Education in France was under Church control, essentially religious in content, inspiration, and direction. The bishop was the local superintendent of public instruction, acting through an appointed superintendent of schools who was mainly involved with the financial concerns of the individual teachers under his patronage.

The Council of Trent had mandated free parish schools (on the primary level) for the poor, establishing the parish priest as the new and sole authority overseeing the poor's religious instruction and schooling in his parish. In response to this mandate, numerous parish-based "charity schools" were established with mixed success. Parish priests could now open their own schools, but anyone else had to have the superintendent's permission to open or teach in a primary school. Qualifications among primary teachers varied widely. Often they were tradesmen (cobblers, tailors, rope or candle makers, and so on) who gave some daily time to instructing children, and receiving a little extra income as a result. Claude Joly, the superintendent of schools in Paris in the latter part of the 17th century, was accused of employing "low pot-house-keepers, barbers, flunkeys, fiddlers, and marionette string-pullers"[5] in his Little Schools. Lay teachers were rarely, if ever, trained as such, and although they were exempt from certain taxes and military service, their fixed salary paid by the foundation sponsoring the school had to be supplemented by small monthly fees paid by students based upon how many subjects they took. Most parish schools continued to suffer from a lack of adequately trained full-time teachers, sufficient money, and appropriate school buildings.

By the time De La Salle became involved in primary education in 1680, primary schools were plentiful, although widely divergent in style and quality. Primary schooling consisted of learning the main essentials of education, up to the age of nine. Reading was begun with Latin syllables and words, the theory being that these were easier to learn and more beneficial besides, and after primary school, a male student would be ready to enter a college where his education would continue in Latin.

Those first years of one's education—experienced almost exclusively by boys—could be acquired in various ways, based on one's social status and financial means:

- **Being Tutored at Home.** This was the preferred option of the wealthy. It was also the way that De La Salle himself was educated.

- **Attending a Grammar School.** These were primary schools connected with some university. It was presumed that a boy's education would be continued at the connected university afterwards.

- **Attending Choir School.** Those singing in the cathedral choir attended their own school on the cathedral grounds.

- **Attending a "Little School."** These were taught by schoolmasters who belonged to the Guild of Schoolmasters. They were paid a modest fee by the parents and were supervised by the diocesan superintendent of schools.

- **Attending a Convent School.** These were boarding and day schools taught by nuns. Such schools were the exclusive domain for girls and an income resource for convents.

- **Attending a Writing School.** Fee-based and focused on learning methods of handwriting, these schools were taught by the Guild of Writing Masters, officially protected by the civil authorities. Along with writing and reading, such schools also taught bookkeeping.

- **Attending a Charity School.** These schools, operated by the poor house (aka the General Hospice or General Hospital) or by a parish, were for the destitute; that is, those officially listed as "the poor" in a parish.

- **Other Small Single Schools.** These were educational ventures sponsored by a city, religious order, pious group, abbey or the like, that generally had a specific focus, clientele, or philosophy. They often remained local and limited in scope or history, not lasting longer than the first generation of teachers. (The schools that De La Salle and the Brothers first established could be considered as part of this group, beginning as a particular kind of "charity school" that reached out to a much wider public, introducing the new category of "Christian Schools.")

The poor in the towns and cities, however, would rarely attend any of these schools, even the charity schools. A non-working child represented a lack of income to the family, and there was little relationship between the subjects studied in most schools and the daily concerns of poor working people.

The Little Schools and charity schools were schools that provided a terminal education. An average stay at these schools lasted two or three years. With some knowledge of reading, writing,

arithmetic, manners, and religious instruction, students were then apprenticed to various trades or found work as they could. Those tutored at home or taught in grammar schools attached to universities were expected to continue their education, pursuing either law, medicine, or a Church position.

Pedagogy

On the primary level, education involved rote memorization and the individual recitation of lessons to the teacher. While other students were

Before John Baptist de La Salle's approach, the schoolmaster would teach only one pupil at a time, as shown in this engraving by Abraham Bosse.

either studying, engaged in some manual task, or creatively interacting with each other (gambling was very popular), one student would be with the teacher, displaying his knowledge of the assignment. Very often, a single room with benches and tables was the school—either a room in the teacher's house, one rented for the purpose, or a place supplied by the authorities. About 20 students made up a school, all bringing their own books and writing materials. There were no charts or blackboards since individual instruction was the norm.

Few schools taught writing, and those that did so, taught writing in Latin, almost always in the schools for the more wealthy. Part of De La Salle's genius was in "pushing the envelope" when it came to teaching writing, a skill that was closely guarded as the exclusive domain of the Guild of Writing Masters. But De La Salle realized that "unless the *petites écoles* offered something more than religious education, parents would not send their children to school—hence its strongly vocational focus. In the great majority of schools, 'reading' literacy rather than 'writing' literacy was the priority."[6] But De La Salle knew that writing was a transformative skill, and that "the child that knows how to read and write will be capable of anything."[7] So in his schools, the teaching of writing would happen despite the political implications among those who thought they had a monopoly in that area.

In the schools of the time, all ages and abilities were taught in the same room. Some of the schools were open only in winter, others for only three or four days a week. Attendance was generally inconsistent, depending on the disposition of the students or the teacher on any particular day. Corporal punishment was considered a normal part of effective instruction. Even the king had been subject to such methods by his early teachers.

The teachers who staffed the schools were little trained in pedagogy. Those staffed by clergy from recently introduced seminary training programs at least benefited from their intellectual formation, even if these clerics-in-training had never been instructed in the art of teaching or classroom management. In almost all the schools in France, there was no organized system for selecting, training, and supervising the teachers after they had entered the classroom. Besides, lay teachers taxed the parish's financial resources, and retaining them was difficult, since someone sufficiently prepared to teach in the charity school could easily make more money in some other occupation. Some had tried to establish religious congregations or confraternities dedicated to teaching boys, but none met with much success until the work of De La Salle and his Brothers.

Recognize Jesus beneath the poor rags of the children whom you have to instruct. Adore him in them. — *Meditation 96.3*

De La Salle's Educational Philosophy

De La Salle's genius lay in developing ways to organize schools, to train and supervise teachers, and to adapt various educational methodologies in addressing immediate local needs, thereby elevating the ministry of teaching by laymen within the Church. What had been done poorly by others was now being done well by them. Both the religious convictions which led him and his Brothers to see Christ in the poor, and the empathy which drew him into for the ministry of educating the poor, provided the foundation upon which his developed understanding of the vocation of the Christian teacher was progressively built.

One of his written meditations expresses this well, as it paints a stark contrast between 1) the poor and 2) God's universal love. It was those two specific juxtaposed realities—called De La Salle's "double contemplation" by some scholars today—which became the catalyst for the genesis of the Christian Schools. De La Salle discovered his own vocation, his life's work, when he saw that it was he and those who joined him who could, and should, live out God's providential care for those whose education was entrusted to their care. The following meditation that he wrote for the Brothers gives a good, succinct description of how he looked upon this ministry, and how he saw the vocation of the Brothers as a manifestation of God's providential care for those most in need:

Consider that it is a practice only too common for working people and the poor to allow their children to live on their own, roaming all over like vagabonds, as long as they are unable to put them to some work. These parents have no concern to send their children to school, because their poverty does not allow them to pay teachers, or else, obliged as they are to look for work outside the home, they have to abandon their children to fend for themselves.

The results of this condition are regrettable, for these poor children, accustomed to lead an idle life for many years, have great difficulty adjusting when it comes time for them to go to work. Furthermore, through association with bad companions, they learn to commit many sins that are very difficult to stop later on because of the persistent bad habits they have contracted over such a long time.

God has had the goodness to remedy so great a misfortune by the establishment of the Christian Schools, where the teaching is offered free of charge and entirely for the glory of God, where the children are kept all day, learn reading, writing, and their religion, and are always busy, so that when their parents want them to go to work, they are prepared for employment.

Thank God, who has had the goodness to employ you to procure such an important advantage for children. Be faithful and exact to do this without any payment, so that you can say with Saint Paul, The source of my consolation is to announce the Gospel free of charge, without having it cost anything to those who hear me.[8]

The inner court of the De La Salle house in Reims. This is a 19th century engraving by Joffroy of a drawing by Fichot. It would have been here that the family's children would often play.

THE EARLY YEARS

John Baptist de La Salle, called Jean-Baptiste in his native tongue, was the first of 11 children born to Louis de La Salle, who was a magistrate in the présidial court of Reims, and Nicolle Moët de Brouillet. Two younger sisters and two younger brothers died in infancy, something not uncommon at the time. The city of Reims, with its narrow streets, multiple churches, and large central cathedral, was home to an extended family of aunts, uncles, cousins, and grandparents. From the time he was born on April 30, 1651, to the time the family moved several blocks away 13 years later, John Baptist grew up in a stately residence near the center of this city of kings and merchants, in a house that exists to this day. The courtyard and the street recess leading to the family home were the places where he played with his siblings, and the house with its Renaissance façade was the place where he first learned how to read and write, under the direction of a tutor. The nearby cathedral with its echoing ancient bells dominated the skyline as it dominated the pious practices of his family.

Family Influences

With relatives associated with both the cathedral and with various religious orders, John Baptist's religious upbringing was thoroughly assured. At the same time, his upper-class family maintained a lifestyle in keeping with their station, employing servants and entertaining guests on a regular basis. While not pampered, one may assume that John Baptist led a comfortable existence, encountering none of the difficulties experienced by the poor or the destitute. During those initial years, it became evident that John Baptist had inherited the integrity and professional seriousness of his father and the human qualities and virtues of his mother, who had been brought up in the most

The cathedral of Reims, which was still under construction during De La Salle's lifetime, although many parts of it were finished and used. He served as a canon here for 16 years. The painting is by Dominico Quaglio (1787-1837).

exacting practices of Christian piety. Whether true or not, one account of his early life portrays the young John Baptist as someone who would rather listen to his grandmother read from the *Lives of the Saints* than join the family's musical soiree downstairs. We do know that he had a pious disposition and a quiet, studious personality.

A painting of the 16–18-year-old John Baptist de La Salle as a young canon of the Reims Cathedral.

Education

It was generally expected that the eldest son of Louis de La Salle would follow in his father's footsteps with a law career. But from his youth, John Baptist had been attracted to the life of the Church. After four years of tutoring at home, having learned how to read and spell from Latin texts, he was enrolled in the *Collège des Bons-Enfants,* an adjunct school of the University of Reims, in October of 1661. Near the end of his first year at the Collège, at the tender age of 10, John Baptist decided to officially aspire to the priesthood. At the invitation of his distant cousin, Father Pierre Dozet, chancellor of the university, he took part in a ceremony that included the cutting off of a small piece of his hair, called a clerical tonsure, to show his intention of becoming a priest. Afterwards, now wearing the black cassock, John Baptist continued to excel in his prescribed course of classical studies.

Some years later, in 1666, when John Baptist was almost 16, Pierre Dozet again favored his young cousin by resigning his own Church appointment as "canon" (someone with specific cathedral-related duties and benefits) of the Reims cathedral and transferring the position to him—something you could do in the society of the time. The teenager would now be a member of a very exclusive community of over 60 clerics who "staffed" the famous cathedral of Reims, where the kings of France were anointed. This was a social, religious, and financial jackpot. The position came with regular stipends, fancy dress, honors, processions, and all sorts of other advantages. Among other things, the position obligated him to attend daily Office (sets of public prayers said at different times of the day) and daily Mass, and to participate in regular meetings of the Cathedral Chapter, the group of those who advised the archbishop. Besides the honor and significant financial benefits of this added responsibility, a distinguished position such as this placed John Baptist on the fast track in ecclesiastical circles.

One year later he completed his classical studies at the *Collège des Bons-Enfants* and began the traditional two-year course in philosophy. These studies were completed on July 9, 1669, when he passed a long oral examination (in Latin) on logic, ethics, and philosophy with highest honors. At 18 years of age, he was now ready to enter the university, carrying with him a master of arts degree, minor orders towards the priesthood, and the benefits associated with membership in the Reims Cathedral Chapter.

After spending one year studying theology at the University of Reims, John Baptist moved to the Seminary of Saint Sulpice in Paris, which was several days travel (95 miles) away from the city of his birth and early life. This seminary had as its goal to produce priests committed to a life of self-sacrifice and self-discipline, with zeal for the salvation of souls, especially the poor. Life was rigorous, filled with work, prayer, and silence. In fact, the overall routine of the seminary—silence, meditation, spiritual reading, reading at meals, daily examination of conscience, multiple devotions, and openness to one's spiritual director, to name a few—bears a striking resemblance to the routine that John Baptist would later introduce in the training of his own schoolmasters, the Brothers.

A portrait of Nicole Moët de Brouillet, De La Salle's mother. She died at the age of 38 and was the mother of 11 children, seven of whom survived infancy.

Family Responsibilities

Soon, however, any expectations he had of leading a fairly ordinary life as a student cleric came to an end. John Baptist's mother died in the final weeks of his first year in Paris and his father died less than nine months later. He wasn't able to get back in time for either funeral; by the time the news reached him, they would already have been buried. As the eldest in the family and the executor of his father's estate, he now quickly returned to Reims to take care of his siblings and the family's business affairs. Upon his arrival back in Reims, he sought out as a spiritual director Father Nicolas Roland, a priest and fellow canon at the cathedral in Reims who was eight years older than he was. Following Roland's advice, John Baptist finished his seminary studies at the University of Reims, and just two months after the death of his father, he was ordained as a sub-deacon, one of the steps toward priesthood. Despite all of the setbacks, he would continue on the path God had placed in his heart.

But the family would not remain together as before. A few weeks after this ordination, his older sister, along with his two-year-old youngest brother, went to live with his maternal grandmother. His other sister had entered the Canonesses of St. Augustine, a semi-contemplative religious order. So the 21-year-old John Baptist was left in charge of his three other brothers who were aged thirteen, eight, and six.

A time of study and domestic responsibilities followed, with John Baptist overseeing the education of his brothers while also doing his own studies.

Ordination to the Priesthood

Six years later, in 1678, John Baptist had achieved a Licentiate in Sacred Theology, and at the end of Lent, on Holy Saturday, April 9, 1678, he was ordained to the priesthood by Charles-Maurice Le Tellier, the Archbishop of Reims. Just shy of 26 years old, he had finally reached the goal that he had set out to obtain some 16 years earlier. He had done so in circumstances he could never have foreseen but through which he had persisted. Little did he know that the adventure of his life's journey had barely begun.

John Baptist, now called Father De La Salle, no doubt saw before him a marginally successful career as a well-regarded cleric in the Diocese of Reims. But it was not to be that predictable. Less than three weeks after his priestly ordination, his spiritual director and friend, Nicolas Roland, died rather suddenly at the age of 35. De La Salle was one of the designated executors of his will. Among other things, the newly ordained 27-year-old was charged with completing Roland's negotiations for securing *letters patent* for the Sisters of the Holy Child Jesus, a religious order Roland had established for the education of poor girls, and to provide what support he could for them. Over the course of a year, De La Salle did just that, getting

De La Salle meeting Adrien Nyel for the first time at the door of the convent of the Sisters of the Child Jesus in Reims. The painting is from Gaveau's 1886 Life of the Founder and is based on an engraving by Gerlier.

the support of the archbishop and others for this new order, and learning in the process which pastors, officials, and leading figures of Reims were the most helpful in solidly establishing this new educational project in his native town. De La Salle also came to advise these religious women on temporal matters and provided for their spiritual needs. His life was now busy with the daily five or six hours at prayer as canon of the cathedral, the priestly ministry of celebrating daily Eucharist and hearing confessions, supporting the sisters in whatever ways they desired or required, providing hospitality to visiting or needy clerics at his family home, and continuing to oversee the family's practical and financial affairs.

Then he met Adrien Nyel.

As for myself, I do not like to make the first move in any endeavor... I leave it to Divine Providence to make the first move and then I am satisfied. — Letter 18

Don't let slip the opportunities that come your way, but don't be overeager. — Letter 24

Do not have any anxiety about the future. Leave everything in God's hands for he will take care of you. — Letter 101

Adrien Nyel

First, a little back story. Nicolas Roland's congregation of teaching sisters had been modeled on the successful work of Father Nicolas Barré and his religious sisters in Rouen, 140 miles west of Reims.

That work was supported by the generosity of a Madame Maillefer, a relative by marriage to the De La Salle family. Adrien Nyel, an administrator at the General Hospice of Rouen (the place that provided various social services for the poor of the area, including education), had been recruiting young men with Barré's help for the education of the poor boys of Rouen. In March of 1679, Adrien Nyel showed up at the convent door of the Sisters of the Holy Child Jesus in Reims with a message from Madame Maillefer that the education of poor boys in her hometown of Reims should be provided for, and he had been engaged by Madame Maillefer to do so. Providentially, De La Salle arrived at the same time that Nyel did.

Inside, they were introduced to each other and after some discussion De La Salle invited Nyel to stay at his house to work out strategies for accomplishing this new educational project. Providentially for Adrien Nyel, De La Salle was the right person in the right place at the right time. They consulted with experienced clerics and local pastors over the next several weeks, many of whom De La Salle had been able to size up because of his earlier work on behalf of Roland's Sisters. Eventually, it was determined that given the legal boundaries governing education at the time, the school should be a parish school and therefore solely under the authority of a local pastor. This would cause the least opposition by the various guilds and others in town who might object to yet another school competing for pupils and funds.

And so a few weeks later, a school was established at the local parish of Saint Maurice, whose pastor was devoted to his parish and who strongly defended his rights in anything that he did for them. De La Salle thought that would be the end of his involvement in the project. Soon, however, another wealthy widow wanted to endow a similar school for her own parish in Reims, but only if De La Salle was involved in the contract and promised to provide some supervision. Reluctantly, De La Salle gave his support. Nyel now had teachers for two schools housed at Saint Maurice, taxing the resources and goodwill of the pastor. De La Salle once again solved the problem by helping to pay for the teachers' upkeep. But by December even that financial help wasn't enough. De La Salle now decided that it was better to rent a house near his house and invited Nyel and his teachers to be based there. Before long, because of Nyel's enthusiasm, the parish in which this particular house was located also opened its own school. However, while he apparently was great at establishing schools, Adrien Nyel was not very good at controlling or inspiring them. Most of the teachers he hired had little training and less supervision.

Living with the Teachers

De La Salle felt responsible and, with the approval of his three younger siblings who still lived with him, he decided that the best thing to do was to have the teachers join him for the daily meals in his nearby home, beginning at Easter of 1680. In this way, he might work more closely with them in becoming better teachers, and perhaps also improve their conversation skills and table manners. He had promised to oversee the investment of those who had provided the funds for these schools, and this was the only way he could see himself fulfilling that promise. His involvement was still wholly external, yet his sense of responsibility led him, in his words, to try "to see to it that they carried out their duties in a religious and conscientious manner."[9] In an interesting twist, at the same time as De La Salle was personally and directly supporting the work of these barely literate "teachers," he was completing his own doctorate in theology at the University of Reims.

The following year saw the three initially successful schools further suffer from Nyel's frequent absences, the lack of any uniform school policy or method, and the increasing need for discipline among the students and teachers. Proactive once again, De La Salle gave the teachers a retreat in his home during Holy Week of 1681, providing them with a spiritual vision of their work, and instilling in them a sense of personal discipline. Nyel was absent, negotiating the opening for yet another school outside of Reims. But when he returned, the change in the teachers was obvious to him, and Nyel may have seen that the young De La Salle had a real future in this ministry of education.

De La Salle gradually realized that without further personal input, matters would quickly revert to the way they had been before. He consulted with Nicolas Barré in Paris, who knew both Nicolas Roland and Adrien Nyel and was actively involved in the cause of education for the poor. The highly regarded priest quickly measured up both De La Salle and the situation and he told him in no uncertain terms to bring the teachers into his house and to live with them full time.

It was radical advice on many fronts. Such a move would have clear consequences in terms of his family (he was the guardian of his younger brothers), his place in society and the Church (the mixing of social classes in this way was not done), and his future plans (any thought of ecclesiastical advancement would, at least, have to be put on hold). This would be a pivotal decision in his life. He prayed about this deeply, and he extensively consulted with others. In the end, De La Salle became convinced that this was the will of God for him. Once convinced, he moved forward without hesitation.

On June 24, 1681, when the lease on the rented house ran out, these simple teachers who were of a social class entirely removed from De La Salle's moved into the house where De La Salle and his family had lived since he was 13 years old. As the oldest in the family, there was little that his siblings and extended family could do to oppose his determined stance, although they certainly tried. One aunt who was present described the scene: "Monsieur De La Salle being the eldest, the family met sometimes at his house for a meal, to keep the union between them...The man of God, who took first place there, needed to arm himself with all his patience to withstand all the things that the family said to him during those meals on the folly they claimed he was committing in undertaking to train masters for the schools to the detriment of his family...When they began to tackle him on that score, he quietly folded his arms, listening patiently to the reasons they alleged from one side or another so as to get him to desist from his undertaking, and answered not a word."[10]

De La Salle could be quite stubborn, apparently, about these kinds of decisions. When it became clear to them that he would not change his mind, despite their interventions and strong protests, it was decided that one of his younger brothers would go to live with their older married sister, and the youngest would go to a boarding school. De La Salle's other brother, 18-year-old Jean-Louis, who would eventually become a priest himself, decided to stay at the house with his brother and the schoolteachers. His brother-in-law, Jean Maillefer, in the name of the family, also sued him for the house, which was part of their shared inheritance, and this lawsuit eventually succeeded, making the new arrangement in the family home rather short-lived.

Never speak to anyone except with kindness, and if you fear to speak otherwise, keep silent.

— *Meditation 96.3*

Formation of Teachers

Through the adoption of a uniform schedule for both house and school, the practice of common religious exercises and ascetical practices, and the inclusion of practical and consistent educational methods, De La Salle strove to slowly form this group of teachers with a common spirit and purpose. According to Dom Maillefer, his nephew and one of his early biographers, De La Salle "was content to lead the teachers by the hand, so to speak, to let them see from their own experience and from his exhortations and example what was the best course to follow."[11] While Adrien Nyel spent his time working on new foundations in cities outside of Reims, De La Salle now directed the teachers and the schools in Reims. From the one central house in the city, teachers left each morning and afternoon to staff the three schools, sharing their experiences upon their return and discussing successes and mistakes with De La Salle who listened and dispensed what advice he could.

The relationship between De La Salle and Adrien Nyel, who was 38 years older than he was, seems to have been generally amiable and mutually supportive but never truly complementary. Nyel had a passion and ability for starting schools. De La Salle acquired a passion for directing and establishing them as solid Christian Schools staffed by dedicated and religiously motivated teachers. At the end of the first six months of living together at De La Salle's house, Nyel left to establish yet another school in the town of nearby Rethel—an effort in which De La Salle had taken charge of the arrangements. Nyel didn't return to Reims for four years, establishing still further schools staffed by teachers that he recruited. Some of these new schools also acquired teachers trained by De La Salle in Reims. The contrast between these teachers and Nyel's recruits, in terms of piety and discipline, was startling to those supporting the new schools. It became clear to both De La Salle and Adrien Nyel that their gifts lay in different directions.

Transition from Teachers to Brothers

De La Salle was becoming involved more deeply at every turn. In June of 1682, a year after the teachers had moved in with him, he had to move out of his family home because the house was lost at auction following the lawsuit pursued by his brother-in-law. But he was now not to be dissuaded from the good work that he had undertaken. The schoolteachers, along with his brother Jean-Louis, moved with De La Salle to a rented double house on *Rue Neuve,* a decidedly poorer section of Reims. The house they moved to would come to be known as the "cradle of the Institute" because it was the first independent location for this new movement, and in fact there is a Lasallian school there to this day. Besides changing houses, De La Salle changed social milieus. Instead of richly appointed spacious rooms, there would be cramped quarters. Instead of everyday servants, refined conversations, delicate aromas, and fine foods, there would be no servants, simple speech, questionable smells, and coarse food. At this new location, the men with De La Salle began to be called "Brothers" instead of "the schoolteachers who live with the priest De La Salle."

From the first, De La Salle was the superior of the group and, by their request, their spiritual director. In a notable exception to most other religious communities of the time, nothing was introduced by authority. Instead, "he flattered them by giving them the satisfaction of being themselves the creators of their own vision and their own plans for making it a reality. In this way they became, in effect, their own legislators."[12] Within six months at the new place, however, the novelty had worn off and all but a few of the original group had left, something De La Salle didn't oppose once it became clear that they weren't cut out for teaching or community life. But new recruits soon arrived who were better disposed for the life that De La Salle was proposing.

Even with these new recruits and the success of the schools, De La Salle's own commitment continued to be challenged, and at a very personal level. Although both the schools and the Brothers' community life were more stable, the Brothers had also become confident enough to question De La Salle's basically secure, upper class life, when compared to their own basically insecure one. Inevitably, circumstances arose when that contrast would come to the surface.

Renunciation of Wealth

One day, when the poverty of their community life had become particularly difficult, he decided to inspire them with a talk that urged them to trust in God's providential care. The talk is recounted by another early biographer who had known and lived with him. The text was very likely taken from De La Salle's own Memoir of the Beginnings, a document that De La Salle had privately written in 1694 but which was lost during the French Revolution. This is what he said to them:

Men of little faith, he said, by your lack of trust you set limits to a goodness that has no limits in itself. If that goodness is indeed infinite, universal, and continual—as you do not doubt— it will always take care of you and never fail you… Consider the lilies of the field, for it is Jesus Christ himself who urges you to reflect on them and on the wild flowers of the countryside and to see how richly God has adorned them and made them beautiful. They lack nothing, yet Solomon himself in all his glory was less splendidly attired. Open your eyes and see the birds that fly through the air or the little animals which creep upon the ground; not a single one of them lacks what is needed. God provides for their necessities.… Therefore, stir up your trust in the Lord's infinite goodness and honor God by leaving in the divine hands the care of your persons. Be not troubled about the present or disquieted about the future, but be concerned only about the moment you must now live. Do not let anticipation of tomorrow be a burden on the day that is passing. What you

lack in the evening, the morrow will bring you,
if you know how to hope in God...[13]

Trusting in God might be a strong regular theme
in De La Salle's talks to them, but the theme of his
family fortune and social position in society spoke
more convincingly. The teachers didn't remain
passive. They replied very directly and candidly.
"It's easy for you to talk," they told him.

> *You have everything you need. You are a rich
> canon with a regular source of income and a
> guaranteed inheritance. You don't know what
> it is to have to do without. If our enterprise falls
> apart, you will survive and the collapse of our
> situation will not involve your own. But we are
> without property, without income, and we don't
> even have a marketable skill. Where will we go
> or what will we do if the schools fail and the
> people no longer want us? The only thing we
> will have left is our poverty and the only solu-
> tion will be to go out and beg.*[14]

Here were words that struck home. Instead of responding as most people would to this sort of challenge—"Look at all I've given you, how much time
and effort I've put into this whole thing!"—he instead
wrote, "I have been reduced to silence. As long as
I am not poor myself, I have no right to speak the
language of perfection."[15] The conversion of his life,
which had begun with the chance encounter with
Adrien Nyel, now reached evermore deeply into
previously unchallenged dimensions of his life.

A 1901 painting by Giovanni Gagliardi (1860-1908) that shows De La Salle distributing bread to the poor during the fierce winter of 1683-1684. This is how he disposed of his share of the family fortune in order to be poor like his Brothers.

De La Salle listened and responded in the same way he would respond in all times of decision: by seeking God's will through prayer, fasting, consultation, reflection, openness to those around him, and resolute but prudent action.

His response was as uncompromising as his developing character. In August of 1683, he resigned his canonry, that lucrative and distinguished position he held at the Reims Cathedral. When he wrote out for himself the reasons why he was making this move, the last of the 10 points listed typifies his approach to the discernment of God's will: "Since I no longer feel myself drawn to the vocation of a canon, it seems to me that this particular vocation has already left me long before I have abandoned it. This state in life is no longer for me. Although I entered it freely through an open door, it seems to me that today God is opening the door again so that I can leave it."[16]

After losing the significant income from his appointed position at the cathedral, his other financial assets remained to be dealt with. Instead of endowing the schools—the natural expectation—De La Salle resisted the idea of endowing the schools on anything less than God's Providence, praying, "If you endow them, they will be well endowed; if you do not endow them, they will stay without endowment."[17] During the great winter famine of 1683-1684, De La Salle saw the opportunity to dispose of his fortune and used it to distribute food daily to all who were in need. W.J. Battersby, FSC, a later biographer of De La Salle, writes:

From all the surrounding countryside beggars flocked into the town in search of food, and the townsfolk themselves were driven to the extremity of misery by the scarcity and high cost of provisions. All he had to do, therefore, was to stand at the door of his house each day and distribute bread to those who wanted it. It soon became known that food was to be obtained for the asking and his house was besieged. At the same time he reserved a certain amount for the famished children in his schools.[18]

We can't say exactly how much De La Salle gave away. One modern estimate puts the amount at about 9,000 livres, which would be around $375,000 in today's currency, and an even higher relative value in the society of the time. As a financial context, we do know that he kept enough to provide himself

---

"Example makes a much greater impression on the mind and heart than words. This is especially true of children, since they do not yet have the minds sufficiently able to reflect, and they ordinarily model themselves on the example of their teachers. They are led more readily to do what they see done for them than to carry out what they hear told to them, particularly when the words they hear are not in harmony with the actions they see." — Meditation 202.3

---

with a basic annual income of 200 livres (about $8,300 today), the standard salary for teachers.

Trust in Providence

The Brothers themselves were amazed at De La Salle's reaction to their outspoken challenge, but they could hardly fault him for responding with such trust in God. Yet now that everyone was reduced to poverty, their insecurity stood out all the more. De La Salle urged them to look about them and see that while many rich merchants and well-to-do religious communities had been ruined by the famine, they who were now without capital or revenue had never lacked the basic necessities. This reliance on God's Providence through poverty was something that he would maintain throughout his life, writing later on that the Brothers would survive only as long as they remained poor; they would lose "the spirit of their state" once they began to get used to comforts beyond what was needed to support their basic needs.

In 1685, the schools that Adrien Nyel had started in other towns were fully placed in De La Salle's care as the 60-year-old Nyel decided, despite De La Salle's attempts to change his mind, to return to Rouen and work in the General Hospice from where he had come six years earlier. But Nyel's energies and enthusiasm were on the decline. When he died two years later of lung disease, De La Salle and the Brothers deeply mourned his death.

Commitment

Now the entire community and all seven schools under their care were in De La Salle's hands. As their public posture increased, their commitment consolidated with the adoption of a common form of dress, called "a poor and modest habit" that caused more than a little ridicule and mockery over the years, and a name, "Brothers of the Christian Schools." At a general assembly of 12 of the principal Brothers, held in 1686, and after a spiritual retreat led by De La Salle, the habit and name were officially adopted. In defining themselves as brothers to one another and older brothers to the young people confided to them by God, they stated both their identity and their mission. At the same time, it was decided that the drafting of an official rule of life would be deferred in order to learn from further experience. The assembled Brothers decided to take a private vow of obedience for three years, renewable annually—it became a sort of "rolling" commitment—and they did so with De La Salle on Trinity Sunday 1686. The next day they made a 27-mile pilgrimage to the shrine of Our Lady of Liesse where they renewed this vow of obedience and entrusted their future to Mary.

Do you have a faith that is such that it is able to touch the hearts of your students and inspire them with the Christian spirit? This is the greatest miracle you could perform and the one that God asks of you, for this is the purpose of your work. — Meditation 139.3

Development and Expansion

As month followed month, the Brothers' sense of community and communal mission became ever stronger. Repeated requests to take over rural schools had to be denied since they had adopted the policy of never sending fewer than two Brothers to a given school and since rural pastors could hardly pay for the support of even one teacher. But this didn't mean that De La Salle wouldn't find some way of addressing this obvious educational need: the training of non-Brother teachers for the rural schools could be accomplished. This became a work in which De La Salle would always remain interested. In 1687, he began to take in young men from the villages within the diocese of Reims, chosen and sent by their rural parish priests for training as teachers. He housed the first group of 25 in a building adjacent to that occupied by the Brothers. De La Salle oversaw their formation as Christian educators while these teachers in training shared a number of common activities with the Brothers. In one sense, the job was done too well. After a few of these groups from the outlying parishes had been trained, no further teachers were needed for the country schools, and that particular enterprise came to an end. Later, such training schools were established again as the need arose.

The following year, in 1687, after the Brothers' retreat preceding Trinity Sunday, De La Salle insisted that the Brothers elect one of their own as superior. Reluctantly, the Brothers elected Brother Henri L'Heureux. De La Salle was the first to kneel and offer obedience to the new superior. But once they heard about this rather unique development, diocesan officials reacted far less favorably, unable to accept or fathom this sort of submissive arrangement of a cleric and former canon of the Cathedral to a Brother. Before long, with a direct order from Archbishop Le Tellier, De La Salle was obliged to resume his place as head of the Society.

After five years of living at *Rue Neuve,* the group had come together with a distinct sense of community, a common vision, a unified method for its successful educational works, and an increasingly clear sense of identity and purpose. Two things are worth noting at this point. First, the community as yet had no *letters patent* and hence enjoyed no legal status. (This was something that De La Salle never actively pursued, and it would not happen until after his death.) The Brothers fell under the jurisdiction of each parish priest in all that concerned the school, although it appears that in the day-to-day running of the group, De La Salle and the Brothers made their decisions with a minimum amount of consultation. Second, De La Salle rarely "opened" a school. He was almost always invited to take over a school situation that already existed but was in desperate need of a new approach. This primary "invitation" approach to new ministries would persist up to the present day, reflecting De La Salle's own trust in God's providential guidance within the events of a person's life.

Role of Women

Another thing worth highlighting at this point is the significant involvement of women in the development of the Lasallian charism. De La Salle's mother, Nicolle Moët de Brouillet, shaped De La Salle's character and piety. His maternal grandmother and godmother, Perette Lespagnol, was very fond of him and a life-long source of guidance and support, from the time when she read to him from the *Lives of the Saints* when he was boy to the time when, at 74 years old, she visited a very ill De La Salle in 1690 at the local Brothers community. Madame Maillefer engaged Adrien Nyel to start the first school, guiding him to the Sisters of the Child Jesus, whose Superior, Françoise Duval, made the connection between Nyel and De La Salle. Catherine des Croyères endowed the second school, meeting with Nyel but insisting to meet with De La Salle, whom she convinced to oversee her investment in the school, and thus getting him truly involved. Then toward the end of his life, it was Sister Louise Hours in Parménie who led him back to the Brothers and to the vocation to which God had called him. These women, and others along the way, were instruments of God's Divine Providence at the founding of the Institute, and women have continued to be key participants in shaping and sustaining its mission.

This engraving shows the country house at Vaugirard that became a retreat and training center for the Brothers. The Founder lived here from 1691 to 1698, and it is where he did much of his writing.

THE MIDDLE YEARS

As the work of the Brothers became a successful religious and educational enterprise, it wasn't long before there were opportunities to spread beyond Reims and its environs. The archbishop in Reims had offered to financially support this new group if they agreed to stay only in his diocese. But in February of 1688, De La Salle and two Brothers traveled to the parish of Saint Sulpice in Paris, whose pastor had been asking him for some years to come and help with the charity school there. This was the same parish and church where he had been in seminary training. The school there exemplified all that was wrong with education. One description is very detailed:

"The morning they first went down to the classrooms to begin their work, the Brothers had quite a shock: there was no order. The doors opened at five 'clock, in the dark. The children turned up as they liked - some two hundred of them eventually. You can imagine the first few arrivals drifting in as they were sent out of the house once their parents were at work, huddling together for the next two or three hours of darkness round the lamp in the classroom,

sleeping, chatting or playing cards and eventu-
ally playing, fighting or gambling in the yard.
The children were dismissed at ten o'clock, and
the doors re-opened from one till four. These
boys were given some training in reading and
writing by [the teacher] and his young assistant,
and then learnt how to knit stockings, gloves
and the like... He sold the articles they made,
partly for his own profit, partly to help the poor.
Now and then [the teacher] gave a religion les-
son. There was no attempt to stop those who
were idle, before and in school, from gambling
with cards and dice."[19]

While not in charge of the school, the Brothers,
through quietly changing what they could within
their own classrooms, soon made an impact. Within a few months, De La Salle was asked to completely take over the school, receiving the funds
to be able to bring two additional Brothers from
Reims. The changes in the school were immediate
and dramatic: a fixed schedule of classes with daily catechism and prayer as a focal point, a fixed
time of coming and going to school (the doors
were locked at all other times), daily attendance
at the parish Mass during the long noon break,
and less emphasis on making and selling stockings, gloves, etc.

Challenges
When they opened another school within the same
parish in 1690, it was legally challenged by the

Masters of the Little Schools, the group of private teachers whose rights were traditionally defended by the diocesan superintendent of schools, Father Claude Joly, who oversaw all 167 Parisian school districts. The Masters alleged that this new school was accepting paying students despite its being a charity school. After an initial victory in the courts, their argument was dismissed on appeal, but the legal battles in Paris were just beginning. The primary reason for such lawsuits was not because De La Salle was teaching the poor, but because he and the Brothers didn't stick to just teaching the poor; i.e., all were welcome and treated equally. Between the Masters of the Little Schools, the Guild of Writing Masters (a sort of union of scribes who exclusively ran writing schools), and the parish-controlled charity schools, each teaching similar subjects in different ways to separate clientele, and each claiming singular privileges, it is little wonder that even the legitimate authorities of the day could scarcely determine their rightful claims to teach certain subjects to certain groups, let alone figuring out how these new "Christian Schools" run by the Brothers fit into the mix.

Challenges came from other quarters as well. The two Brothers who had originally come to Paris with De La Salle didn't agree with some of his decisions and one of them departed as a result. Half the community in Reims left the Society with the remaining eight Brothers thinly stretched among the seven schools of the area. The pastor of Saint Sulpice became uncooperative and was ready to step in and take over. De La Salle and the Brothers in Paris became exhausted with all the work, morale was low all around, and Brother Henri L'Heureux in Reims—on whom De La Salle had placed his hope for taking over the whole enterprise—suddenly became ill and died. Although this last event really hurt him on a deeply personal level, De La Salle looked for and found a Providential dimension to the tragedy. Since Brother Henri had been in training for the priesthood in order to eventually take over as the Superior of the Brothers, De La Salle now discerned that the Society should consist of Brothers alone, and that its non-clerical, exclusively lay dimension was part of the group's essential character, citing both spiritual and practical reasons. They would be Brothers and not priests.

Formation of Brothers

He also found a property on the outskirts of Paris, in Vaugirard, that could become a source of renewal for all of the Brothers, and a novitiate, or training center, for the new candidates. In 1691, he brought everyone there for an extended retreat under his direction. Many of the Brothers had had little in terms of religious formation prior to being put before a classroom of young, street-wise students. When De La Salle realized that more time would be needed for some of them, he prolonged the retreat into the school year, arranging to replace these Brothers in their schools with some of the rural lay teachers he had trained through the Reims teacher training program. This time of retreat was so successful that such periods of religious renewal became a regular part of the Brothers' yearly program.

Eventually, the religious and educational themes that were taken up at these retreats were consolidated in De La Salle's *Meditations for the Time of Retreat,* a pivotal text that brought together many elements of this unique teaching vocation. Significantly, below the title of the original work was the sentence "For the use of all persons who are engaged in the education of youth, and especially for the retreat which the Brothers of the Christian Schools make during the time of vacation." The intended audience was much larger than only the Brothers. Although it was initially written primarily for the Brothers, De La Salle knew that many, including those country school masters he had trained in Reims, would benefit from developing a deeper, religiously centered educational spirituality and thereby profit from the years of shared experience among the Brothers.

For how long has Jesus been presenting himself to you and knocking at the door of your heart, in order to make his dwelling within you, and you have not wanted to receive him. — Meditation 85.1

After this extended time of retreat, the Brothers were instructed to write De La Salle monthly, giving an account of their behavior and their interior dispositions. He faithfully replied to each of these confidential letters. For over 25 years, they were his only link with many of the Brothers. It was in this way that the fervor engendered by the retreat was maintained throughout the year and into the future. The letters both helped the Brothers reflect on their progress in their vocation and kept De La Salle informed as to the state of what was then called the Society. The letters read like a conversation, reflecting a familiar manner. De La Salle's responses were direct and precise, with little if any small talk. Few of the many thousands of letters that De La Salle wrote in this way have survived. The 110 letters to various Brothers that did survive provide one of the more revealing glimpses we have into De La Salle's character.

Rule and Vows

De La Salle also wanted to address the uncertainty and the cumulative challenges that the young community faced now and would continue to face into the future. Choosing two zealous men who seemed to be the most committed to the work, he proposed that they take with him a private vow to establish this Society no matter what might happen.

They did so on November 21, 1691, at Vaugirard. For many years, no one else knew of this vow, later called the "heroic vow" by the Brothers. Although it would be tested in many ways, this declaration of association provided a foundation of intentionality and commitment on which they could build. Perhaps of some significance is the fact that exactly 50 years earlier, on November 21, 1641, Father Jean-Jacques Olier and two of his companions had made a similar private vow at Vaugirard to establish the seminary of Saint Sulpice, the place which came to have such a great influence on De La Salle's personal and spiritual life.

De La Salle began composing an official Rule for the Brothers in the spring of 1694. The draft of this text was submitted to the Brothers with the clear understanding that they would be the ones who would add or subtract items as they saw fit, and they would be the ones who would approve it. This rule of life arising out of the Brothers' common experience took shape throughout De La Salle's lifetime and came to completion only after the General Chapter of 1717. The daily schedule from the years in Reims had been adopted in 1686 and was subsequently modified and developed in the light of the Brothers' experience. When the 1694 Rule was put together, De La Salle's choices were quite eclectic, drawing from many sources but adapting them to their unique life and ministry.

In considering the question of introducing perpetual or life vows, De La Salle and the senior Brothers he consulted proposed making vowed commitments that were specifically d irected to their mission of extending the reign of God through education. And so on June 6, 1694, Trinity Sunday, these 12 Brothers and De La Salle privately made perpetual vows of association to conduct the gratuitous schools, stability in the Society,

An engraving of John Baptist de La Salle writing the Rule of the Brothers. It was done by Auguste-Louis Chapon, based on an 1887 painting by Charles-Louis Müller.

and obedience. When on the following day De La Salle again recommended that the Brothers elect one of their own as Superior, he was promptly and unanimously re-elected, twice (!), much to his consternation. After the Brothers pointed out that this was simply God's will, De La Salle stopped trying to change their minds but had them sign a declaration stating, among other things, that the present election

> *"...will not have the force of a precedent for the future. Our intention is that after the said John Baptist de La Salle, and forever in the future, no one shall be received among us or chosen as Superior who is a priest, or who has received Holy Orders; and that we will not have or accept any Superior who has not associated himself with us, and has not made vows like us and like all those who will be associated with us in the future...."[20]*

The unique character of the Society as an independent, non-clerical, mission-based, communal educational ministry was becoming more and more clear to De La Salle, and he would do all he could to preserve and strengthen that charism.

Consolidation

Now De La Salle and the Brothers began to fortify their Society, consolidating the already flourishing schools and communities, and forming the young candidates asking to join their way of life. De La

Salle focused more on creating a wide variety of written resources, both for the schools and for the Brothers. The breadth and content of these works was truly striking. They included everything from a student reading text on politeness and decorum, to prayers to be said in school, to how to teach French syllables, to three versions of a catechism for three different audiences, to a detailed method for the Brothers' interior prayer, to the very practical and constantly updated "handbook" for running the schools, to a set of pious song texts for students to sing to popular melodies of the day, to meditations for each of the Sundays and feasts of the church year.[21] During the 15 years between 1694 and 1709, new schools were opened

and closed, Brothers joined and left, legal battles with the Writing Masters and the Masters of the Little Schools raged on, and little by little the identity that De La Salle had begun to form among the Brothers took hold.

Expansion and Development

Some of the highlights of those years include the following:

- The Brothers established a Sunday School for Parisian working men under the age of 20 who wished either to continue their education beyond the elementary level or to learn to read and write if they had never attended school. Two of De La Salle's most talented Brothers taught reading, writing, mathematics, draftsmanship, catechism, and art on Sunday afternoons at this "Christian Sunday Academy."

- Schools were established in Chartres where, in response to the bishop's request that the Brothers teach Latin, as other schools did, De La Salle wrote a defense for teaching French, their native language, to students instead of Latin. His reasons? French was much more practical than teaching Latin. French was easier to learn, took less time, was more useful, could be a vehicle for learning Latin, and was

Image - facing page: A pen and ink drawing of a painting by Benjamin Vautier (1829-1898) called "Children Leaving School" with a Brother at the door watching with benign amusement. Two versions of the painting exist. One of them is at the Victoria and Albert Museum (London).

65

a necessary tool for learning other things (including Christian doctrine). Besides the fact that Latin was of little use to working people, there was not enough time to master it in the Christian Schools, and those who knew only a little looked foolish trying to use it.

- One of the "heroic vow" participants, Brother Gabriel Drolin, was sent to Rome with Brother Gérard (who was also his blood brother) to establish a school there. When they arrived, they couldn't speak the language, had few contacts, and found that education for the poor was well provided for. Besides, Rome had a highly organized and clerically dominated school system that showed little interest in any other model of education. Brother Gérard soon returned to France, but Brother Gabriel remained in Rome for 26 years (1702-1728), faithfully struggling to get a foothold in the ecclesiastical school system. He eventually received a license to teach in one of the papal schools and finally established his own school, although he never received a second Brother as De La Salle had so often promised in the letters that we still have. Others eventually did arrive, but only after the death of De La Salle. Today, the schools in Rome credit their foundation to Brother Gabriel Drolin's valiant and long-serving years of ministry.

- Schools were established in other towns and cities, including Calais, Avignon, Marseilles, and Grenoble, each school adopting its own characteristics based on local needs and the likely employment prospects that students would face. At the same time, the pedagogy and methodology were uniform throughout, based on the experiences and lessons learned among the other Christian Schools. When Brothers were moved from one school to another, they could easily pick up where others had left off because of that uniformity.

Do you have these sentiments of charity and tenderness toward the poor children whom you have to educate? Do you take advantage of their affection for you to lead them to God? If you have for them the firmness of a father to restrain and withdraw them from misbehavior, you must also have for them the tenderness of a mother to draw them to you, and to do for them all the good that depends on you. — Meditation 101.3

- The school and community at Saint Sulpice in Paris went through several crises. The archbishop of Paris appointed a new ecclesiastical superior for the Brothers because of a perceived internal disciplinary severity on a part of several Brothers who were in charge. De La Salle accepted this appointment, but the Brothers would have none of it and didn't hesitate in letting this be known, creating quite a stir. Only by means of a compromise did they accept an occasional visit to the house by such an ecclesiastical superior. Then, in 1706, the courts of the Parliament, the major judicial body in Paris, forbade De La Salle and the Brothers "to establish any community under the name of a training school for teachers in the primary schools, or anything similar" in Paris or its environs without the express permission of the diocesan superintendent of schools. The Brothers at the three schools in the parish of Saint Sulpice responded by closing their schools abruptly and leaving Paris virtually overnight. It was only by the direct appeal of the pastor to De La Salle, and his judicious compromise with the authorities, that the Brothers were persuaded to return.

• The Brothers came to take over the four charity schools in Rouen that Adrien Nyel had overseen prior to his involvement with De La Salle. For two years, De La Salle and five Brothers lived in the city's General Hospice, caring for its inhabitants as part of their contract and running the city's charity schools besides. In 1705, they moved to Saint Yon, an extensive property away from the city noise with a manor house, spacious gardens, and a quiet environment. Here the novices were trained, the annual retreat was held, and three new ventures were begun: a boarding school for older boys who were destined for careers in commerce and industry, the first secondary school curriculum of its kind; a house of correction for delinquent children where students were strictly supervised outside of common classes with the other students; and a house of detention for those young men confined by the courts by way of *lettres de cachet*, which were written orders from the king, validated by the royal seal. The Brothers' success in transforming many of their charges outweighed the difficulties and challenges that these new ventures presented, and the income that Saint Yon generated served to support the work elsewhere.

- All of these new foundations, along with the daily concerns that demanded attention, eventually required De La Salle to place a Brother in Avignon who would oversee all the schools in the south, and to have another Brother visit and supervise the schools in and around Reims—hence the term "Visitors" for today's Lasallian provincial superiors. Thus the principle of providing education for the poor "together and by association" was maintained; together in one school community and in association with all those other school communities.

A painting of John Baptist de La Salle teaching class by Cesare Mariani (1826-1901). On the occasion of De La Salle's beatification in 1888, the Institute presented this very large painting to Pope Leo XIII. The painting has been on display from time to time in the Vatican Museum and in the Generalate in Rome.

THE LATER YEARS

At one point in his life, when he was reflecting on the schools and the early years, De La Salle had written that if he had known about all of the difficulties and challenges that lay ahead, he never would have started getting involved in this ministry in the first place. But actually it was now, as he was nearing the age of 60, and after more than 25 years of working with the Brothers, that some of the most difficult hardships were to make their appearance.

The Brothers throughout France suffered with the rest of the population as cold weather, crop failures, and the demands of the War of Spanish Succession (1701-1714) led to a great famine in 1709 with all of its attendant miseries. The novices were moved from Rouen back to Paris for some years so that the Brothers in Rouen might concentrate on their own needs. Many religious orders went bankrupt or were decimated by disease and death, but the Brothers survived, with De La Salle constantly urging them to trust in Providence.

This tremendous trust in God's Providence that De La Salle displayed was neither naive nor falsely pious. He had had too many experiences that confirmed God's continual care for him and for the work of the Brothers. At the same time, De La Salle worked hard to follow through on the direction in which God's will appeared to be leading him. His administrative capabilities were as thorough as they were visionary. While he practiced many penances and encouraged the austere lifestyle of the Brothers, he was also concerned about their well-being, insisting, for example, that the Brothers' houses include a courtyard or a garden where the Brothers could relax and revitalize themselves from the demands of the classroom.

You are under the obligation to instruct the children of the poor. You should, consequently, cultivate a very special tenderness for them and procure their spiritual welfare as far as you will be able, considering them as members of Jesus Christ and his well-beloved. Faith, which should animate you, should make you honor Jesus Christ in their persons, and make you prefer them to the wealthiest children on earth because they are the living images of Jesus Christ our divine Master. By the care you have for them, show how truly dear they are to you. — Meditation 80.3

The reputation of the Christian Schools contin-ued to lead to new foundations in places such as

Versailles and elsewhere, even as legal and ecclesial challenges by pastors and bishops were constantly being met across France. But for De La Salle himself, it was one legal situation that was to precipitate his greatest personal challenge. This is a little complex, but it is worth knowing, since it illustrates several dimensions of De La Salle's character and the historical circumstances within which he lived.

A Legal and Personal Challenge

In 1707, a young well-to-do layman, Jean-Charles Clément, offered to use a substantial part of his allowance to begin a center for the training of country schoolmasters. Despite De La Salle's initial reluctance in the face of both the young man's enthusiasm and the standing court order forbidding him to open any kind of teacher training school within the jurisdiction of the superintendent in Paris, De La Salle held a project such as this close to his heart and, after what can only be termed "nagging" on the part of the young man, eventually provided a substantial down payment in 1708 so that Clément could purchase a property for the training center in Saint Denis, just outside of the Paris jurisdiction. The school opened in 1709 and soon duplicated the success of the earlier teacher training schools that the Brothers had conducted.

Since Clément was legally a minor—under the age of 25—the house had been bought for him by a lawyer, who held a receipt signed by young

Clément assuring De La Salle that he would receive a reimbursement once Clément was given the position by which he would collect the financial benefits associated with the wealthy abbey of Saint Calais, an imminent event. When this position became an actuality in 1710, Clément's attitude suddenly changed, and he refused either to pay back De La Salle or to pay the balance of the purchase price, although strangely Clément insisted that he wanted the house for himself. The picture became more complicated as the original owner tried to get the house back and the lawyer attempted to resell the house to another buyer. Then, once the young man's father, a well-known and well-connected court physician, became involved, the situation grew even worse.

In 1711, after a brief journey to the south of France to visit the Brothers' communities there, De La Salle returned to Paris to find that the Clément family, recently granted noble status by the king, would accept nothing less than his public condemnation in the courts as a criminal who had taken advantage of a minor to advance his own aims. Neither De La Salle's offer to forgive the debt, nor the evidence of the original arrangement, was sufficient to outweigh the fact that Clément had been a minor. The court's judgment was brought against De La Salle on May 31, 1712. Not only did he have to cancel the debt and reimburse Clément for the money Clément had spent in supporting the training center, De La Salle was criminally condemned for trying to extort promises of money and warned to never again enter into business negotiations with minors; i.e., those under 25 years of age. In effect, he was convicted of what today might be called "contributing to the delinquency of a minor," as strange as that might seem given the facts of the case.

When De La Salle found out from his lawyer in January of 1712 that the case against him was lost, that the house at Saint Denis would be confiscated, that the school would be closed down, and that there was a warrant out for his arrest, he decided to leave. (Fleeing the area of a law court's jurisdiction was not an uncommon response at the time, especially given the often compromised "justice" from the courts.) Giving his lawyers all the relevant documents and a detailed memoir on the entire history of the situation, De La Salle left Paris to resume his tour of the south. When the final judgment against him came in May, he was visiting the Brothers in Marseilles and so outside the legal jurisdiction of Paris.

To the Brothers in the north, this was a definite crisis. It seemed to them that De La Salle had abandoned them, leaving so quickly in the face of so many difficulties that they were facing. Actually, De La Salle had left the relatively unknown Director of Novices, Brother Barthélemy, in charge and was doing what he thought best for the Brothers. Perhaps he also believed that it was high time that the Brothers learned how to deal with things on their own.

Barthélemy wrote to all the communities, saying that Monsieur de La Salle was in good health, that he had had to flee, that the place where he had gone was known, and that, according to the intention of their common father, they could write to Barthélemy and he would do what he could to satisfy them. He made clear that he was only a substitute for their real Superior until he returned, that he was not in this position by personal right, and that he would try to govern according to De La Salle's spirit. This clarified the position for most of the other Brothers, and they accepted him on those conditions. It was a touchy thing for them that any Brother would try to take the place of the one they regarded as a saint and as their indispensable Founder. Yet it was time, and past time, for them to face up to having a Brother installed as Superior General before De La Salle died, and to relieve an aging man of the burden.[22]

You have committed yourselves to God in the place of those whom you instruct. By taking upon yourselves the responsibility for their souls, you have, so to speak, offered to him soul for soul. Have you sometimes reflected on the commitment you have made, taking responsibility for those whom God has entrusted to you, in order to be faithful to it? Do you have as much care for their salvation as you have for your own? — Meditation 137.3

De La Salle's second journey to the south of France, beginning in February of 1712, lasted for more than two years. We don't know for certain whether this extended separation from the Brothers in the north was due to the decrease of his influence and an active opposition against him on the part of some Church authorities in Paris, along with the legal decision against him, or to a genuine desire to remove himself from the Brothers' struggles toward independence. From his time in the south of France, however, it appears that he maintained a vigorous interest in both the schools and the religious development of the Brothers and their vocation, with just a few hiccups along the way.

After an initial month's stay visiting the Brothers and notables in Avignon, where the schools had been successfully established since 1703, De La Salle resumed the tour of communities that he had begun a year earlier. Everywhere he went, Brothers, pastors, and bishops treated him with great hospitality and respect, leading De La Salle often to cut short his visits or to depart in secrecy so as to avoid the accolades and honors given to him. During these visits, he would encourage the Brothers in their vocations, urging them to remain faithful to their religious duties. When supporters requested that individual Brothers be permanently assigned to their schools, he would explain the nature of the Society and the importance of the Society's autonomy despite its lack of canonical or legal status. Brothers must be able to be sent wherever they will be able to do the most good.

De La Salle tried to establish a novitiate in Marseilles, but this was not to be and it closed after a short time. Jansenism's hold was too firmly established in the area, and the people could not support the training of candidates who would be assigned to work elsewhere in France. Several Brothers' communities in the area also resisted his efforts at reforming them from the rather easy lifestyle they had gradually adopted.

Estrangement

Believing it best that he leave the Brothers to work things out for themselves, he quietly left Marseilles, climbing a steep 30 miles to the sacred grotto of Sainte Baume, famous as the supposed last place where Mary Magdalene lived. Here he sought God's will in solitude and prayer, as rumors circulated that De La Salle was about to leave the Brothers to the designs of Providence and retire to a remote parish in order to work for the conversion of hardened sinners. After spending some time at Sainte Baume, followed by 40 days of retreat at the nearby monastery of Saint Maximin, he traveled to the community at the town of Mende, where the Brothers had also cultivated an easy lifestyle. De La Salle couldn't budge them an inch, however, and he was further chagrined to find that the community couldn't (or wouldn't) even accommodate him in the Brothers' house. For two months, he stayed first in Mende with the Capuchins and then with Mademoiselle Lescure, the founder of the Ladies of the Christian Union, whom he helped in composing a rule for her teaching institute.

De La Salle became less and less convinced that he should maintain his direction of the Brothers. The Brothers in Paris seemed fine without him, and those in and around Marseilles were little influenced by his advice. When his former Director of the novitiate in Marseilles, Brother Timothy, sought him out at Mlle. Lescure's home to report an empty novitiate and to request a new assignment, De La Salle's response was: "Why do you come to me with all of this? Don't you know that I am not competent to give orders to others? Are you not aware that there are many Brothers who no longer want to have anything to do with me? They say they no longer want me as their Superior. And they are right. I am really incapable of that anymore."[23]

According to an early biographer, "The Brother, who had always kept a tender veneration for his worthy Superior, could not keep back his tears at this talk. He threw himself at his feet and told him he would not abandon him until he let him know his will. De La Salle consoled him and indicated a house where he told him to withdraw while waiting till it pleased God to restore calm to them." Eventually, De La Salle was persuaded by this Brother that he was still very much wanted and needed. He then sent Brother Timothy to the community in Avignon. (This same Brother Timothy was chosen by the Brothers as the Superior General after Brother Barthélemy and served in that role for 31 years, 1720-1751.)

In August of 1713, De La Salle traveled to the Brothers' community in Grenoble, and here he was well received. Choosing an isolated cubicle in the recess of a tower that was part of the house, he remained in solitude and prayer for several months, working on his writings. But when he sent one of the Brothers north to obtain more information about the Brothers' situation there, he took over his classes in the school, regularly leading the children to the nearby church and celebrating Mass for them. The fervor of his piety made a great impression on the people of Grenoble, where he is still esteemed today. But the harsh winter took its toll on his health, and new attacks of rheumatism again threatened his life. The whole city offered prayers for his recovery.

Parménie, the place where John Baptist de La Salle came toward the end of his life and found peace from his difficulties. From here he was called back to resume his work with the Brothers and the Institute. Today it is a Lasallian retreat center.

Resolving to make another spiritual retreat, he went to a hermitage near Grenoble called Parménie. This hermitage had recently been built on the ruins of a medieval monastery. At this retreat center established by a devout and pious visionary named Sister Louise, De La Salle initially stayed 15 days, spending time in conversation with her and subsequently corresponding with her. He would go there whenever a priest friend, who was the chaplain there, needed to be elsewhere. Some think that De La Salle seriously considered retiring at Parménie, perhaps as the resident spiritual director.

Recall by the Brothers in Paris

It was while De La Salle was in Grenoble that he received a letter, dated April 1, 1714, from the Directors and the principal Brothers of the Paris region. The Brothers there had been trying to contact him for a long time, but their letters had either never been delivered or had never been answered by De La Salle. The situation in Paris had become quite difficult due to the increasing influence of the Sulpician pastors in their Society's internal affairs, and due to the need for guidance in many administrative matters that required a clear central authority. In this letter, these Brothers in effect ordered De La Salle to return by virtue of his vow of obedience and to again take up its general government.

Reverend and our very dear Father. We, the leading Brothers of the Christian Schools, having in view the greater glory of God, the greater good of the Church and of our Society,

*acknowledge that it is of extreme consequence
that you should resume the care and the general conduct of the holy work of God which is also
yours, since it has pleased the Lord to make use
of you to found it and to guide it for so long.*

*Everyone is convinced that God gave you and
still gives you the grace and the talents necessary to govern well this new Society, which is
of such great usefulness to the Church, and
we bear you the testimony in all justice that
you have always led it with much success and
edification.*

*And so, Monsieur, we beg you very humbly
and we command you in the name of and on
behalf of the body of the Society to which you
have promised obedience, to take care immedi-
ately of the general government of our Society.*[24]

He asked the advice of Sister Louise, the illit-
erate shepherdess who had rebuilt Parménie and
also had become someone in whom he could
confide. She told him, "It is evident that the Lord
wants you to go back to Paris." His work was not
yet done, and he should respond to this further invitation from God in support of the schools. And
so, on August 10, 1714, after stopping at various
communities along the way, De La Salle arrived
back in Paris, knocked on the door of the Brothers' house, and said to the Brothers, "Well, here I
am. What do you want of me?"

Instead of taking over the day-to-day affairs
of the Society, he let it be known that he would

resume his sacramental ministry only, giving advice where needed or asked for, but that Brother Barthélemy would have to run the Society with the help of the senior Brothers.

"Be satisfied with what you can do, since this satisfies God, but do not spare yourself in what you can do with the help of grace. Be convinced that, provided you are willing, you can do more with the help of God's grace than you imagine."

— Collection of Various Short Treatises

Gradually, De La Salle's experience, demeanor, wisdom, and influence began to stabilize and solve many of the administrative problems that had developed over the last few years. And after a year in Paris, De La Salle had Brother Barthélemy, along with the few novices that remained, return to the Saint Yon property in Rouen, coming there himself a month later. While the new Archbishop of Rouen was less supportive than his predecessor, the parish priests sought De La Salle out for advice on dealing with hardened sinners, and he quickly found himself in continual demand as a confessor and spiritual director.

Leadership Transition

At Saint Yon, De La Salle began to work toward providing for the Society's future stability. His austerities, extensive travel, and recurring illnesses—he was seriously ill for 10 months at Saint Yon—made him and the Brothers realize that they really did need an elected successor who would carry on the work that De La Salle had begun. The clearest choice was Brother Barthélemy, the one who had held the Society together during De La Salle's absence in the south and who now took care of the administrative details.

Toward the end of 1716, with De La Salle now 65 years old, Brother Barthélemy was sent to visit all the houses of the Brothers in preparation for a General Assembly the following year. He did so, traveling for five months and gathering the Brothers' signatures agreeing to the General Assembly. This document with the signatures of the Brothers in the communities of that time has proved to be a valuable source of information, listing all of the early communities and the names of their members. There were at the time 23 communities with 99 Brothers who signed the document, not including De La Salle, Brother Barthélemy, or Brother Gabriel Drolin in Rome.

Sixteen delegates, all Directors of the various houses, gathered at Saint Yon on May 16, 1717. First there were several days of retreat, during which De La Salle spoke to them about the dispositions that they needed to maintain, suggested a way of electing a new Superior, and gave them a prayer that he had composed invoking the assistance of the Holy Spirit. Then he withdrew from the meetings completely, remaining in his room for the duration, so that the Brothers could proceed freely.

Among the decisions that followed, Brother Bar-thélemy was chosen as the new Superior. Discussions about revisions to the Rule of the Brothers took up much of their time. As the end of their agreed-upon time together approached, the multitude of details to be considered led to the decision that De La Salle should prepare a revised version of the Rule based on the Assembly's discussions. The next year, De La Salle completed this revision, adding, among other things, a short section that insisted on the central importance of the Spirit of Faith and Zeal as a fundamental component of the mission of the Institute. This was one of the last things that De La Salle wrote. It is based on his cumulative years of leadership, prayer, and diligence, along with his deep love of God, the Brothers, and the ministry of education. It is worth highlighting the essential parts of this section to the Rule that he added:

> *That which is of the utmost importance, and to which the greatest attention should be given in an Institute is that all who compose it possess the spirit peculiar to it; that the novices apply themselves to acquire it; and that those who are already members make it their first care to preserve and increase it in themselves; for it is this spirit that should animate all their actions, be the motive of their whole conduct; and those who do not possess it and those who have lost it, should be looked upon as dead members… The spirit of this Institute is first, a spirit of faith,*

*which should induce those who compose it
not to look upon anything but with the eyes of
faith, not to do anything but in view of God,
and to attribute all to God... Secondly, the spirit
of their Institute consists in an ardent zeal for
the instruction of children... In order to enter
into this spirit, the Brothers of the Society shall
strive by prayer, instruction, and by their vigi-
lance and good conduct in school, to procure
the salvation of the children confided to their
care, bringing them up in piety and in a truly
Christian spirit, that is, according to the rules
and maxims of the Gospel.*[25]

There was also an added prescription for the
Brothers to read the New Testament daily, "look-
ing upon it as their first and principal rule." This
1718 Rule guided the Institute until 1967 when it
underwent a thorough process of revision in response to the mandates of Vatican Council II.

Move into the Background

Once Brother Barthélemy had been officially
elected as Superior General, De La Salle moved
more and more into the background, referring
all requests for advice or permission to the new
Superior. When in October of 1717, De La Salle
had to go to Paris in order to accept a legacy left
to him by the lawyer involved in the Clément
affair—funds that the lawyer knew had been
unjustly kept from him, and funds that, providentially, now enabled the purchase of the Saint Yon

property in Rouen—he stayed in seclusion at the Seminary of Saint Nicolas du Chardonnet for five months. At this center for clerical renewal and reform, he would not interfere with Brother Barthélemy's new role and would be able to avoid the honors and deference given him by the Brothers. As was the case everywhere he went, his presence at the seminary made a profound impression on the priests and seminarians there.

Upon returning to Saint Yon, De La Salle's greatest satisfaction came from training the novices how to engage in extensive periods of interior prayer. He wrote a treatise on prayer and collected together the various meditations he had been writing over the years for the Brothers' use. His sacramental ministry included the care of the Brothers, the boarding students, and the inmates of the house of detention, taking particular interest in winning over the hardened adults who were in residence there.

Illness and Death

De La Salle became more and more ill in 1719. His rheumatism became chronic and attacks of asthma increased. His head sustained several injuries due to accidents, resulting in continual severe headaches that prevented him from reading and writing. He was gradually confined to bed, too weak to practice his sacramental ministry. The one exception was on March 19th, the Feast of Saint Joseph, who is the special patron and protector of the Institute, when De La Salle

A 1906 painting by Giovanni Gagliardi (1860-1908) of the death of John Baptist de La Salle.

recovered enough to celebrate Mass for the Brothers. He received communion on April 5th, Wednesday of Holy Week, and he was given the sacrament of the sick (called at the time the "last anointing") on Holy Thursday. Toward evening on that day he was able to give the Brothers some final advice, urging them stay together and to avoid too familiar dealings with people of the world because this would lead to disenchantment and the loss of one's vocation. At about midnight, in response to Brother Barthélemy's question as to whether he accepted his sufferings, De La Salle replied with his last words: "Oui, j'adore en toutes choses la conduite de Dieu à mon égard." ("Yes, I adore in all things the conduct of God in my regard." or "Yes, I adore God guiding me in all the events of my life.")

At four o'clock in the morning on Good Friday, De La Salle made an effort to rise from his bed as if to greet someone, then joined his hands, raised his eyes to heaven, and died. His biographer, Canon Blain, wrote, "His face seemed as beautiful and serene after he expired as it had been during his life."[26] He was buried on Holy Saturday in a side chapel of the local parish church, Saint Sever. Since it was Holy Week, the more solemn funeral rituals were delayed until the following week. Throughout Rouen, and soon throughout the Society, word spread that "the Saint is dead." But the extension of his life, work, spirit, and influence was just beginning, eventually reaching further than even his prayers would have been able to imagine.

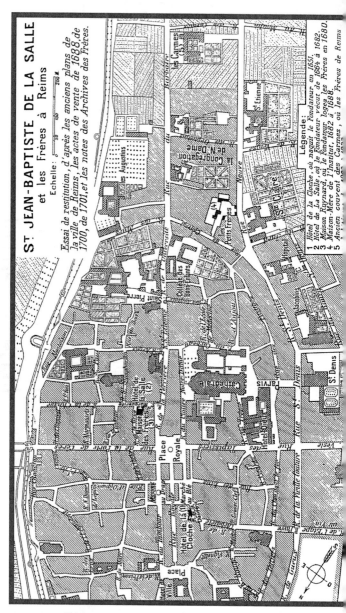

ST JEAN-BAPTISTE DE LA SALLE
et les Frères à Reims

Echelle: 30 100 200 M

Essai de restitution, d'après les anciens plans de la ville de Reims, les actes de vente de 1688, de 1700, de 1701, et les notes des Archives des Frères.

Legende:

1 Hôtel de la Cloche, où naquit le Fondateur en 1651.
2 Hôtel de La Salle, où le Fondateur vécut de 1664 à 1682.
3 Maison Raynard, où le Fondateur logea les Frères en 1680.
4 Maison-Mère de l'Institut, 1682 à 1688.
5 Ancien couvent des Carmes, où les Frères de Reims

This is a reconstructed map of the city of Reims during the time of John Baptist de La Salle. It is based on property records from 1688, 1700, and 1701, along with other documents from the Brothers' archives.

90

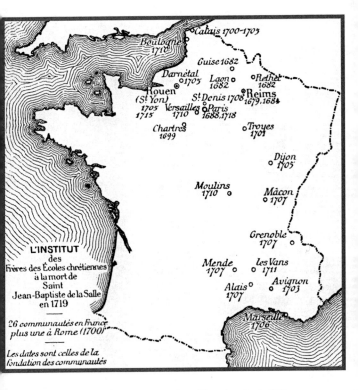

A map of the scope of the Institute and Lasallian education in 1719, when De La Salle passed away. The map shows all of the towns and villages where the Brothers ran schools at that time.

AFTERWORD

Since De La Salle's death in 1719, the Christian Schools that he founded and the Institute of the Brothers of the Christian Schools (De La Salle Christian Brothers) that came about have fluctuated in number as the Brothers expanded throughout France and then throughout the world during the course of the last three centuries. From the 23 communities and some 100 Brothers in 1719, by the time of the French Revolution in the 1790s the group had expanded to over 900 Brothers, almost exclusively in France. But in 1797, the number of Brothers was reduced to less than 40, taking refuge from the French Revolution in Rome. In the 18th and 19th centuries, the Brothers returned to France and grew to over 10,000—also spreading across the globe. In 1965, at their highest number, there were 16,824 Brothers in the Institute.

Other religious orders that were founded in the 18th and 19th centuries happily built on the experience, methodologies, books, and other writings of the De La Salle and the Brothers as their own educational ministries were started and developed. Especially popular were *The Conduct of Christian Schools* and *The Rules of Christian Politeness and Civility*.

Matthew Arnold visited the Lasallian schools in Paris and reported about their methodology to the British House of Commons in 1859. Many female teaching congregations founded in France after the French Revolution adapted the main books written and used by the Brothers, rewriting them for use in the education of girls, as did those teaching congregations originating in Ireland, Scotland, and England. Eventually, those same books came along with the pioneering Sisters who went to Australia and beyond. And Blessed Edmund Rice, the founder of the Brothers of the Christian Schools of Ireland—today called the Congregation of Christian Brothers—incorporated aspects of De La Salle's spirituality, community life, and school organization, having been in contact with the Brothers in France. Hence the writings of De La Salle have been quietly influential in the progress of Catholic Christian education in ways that appear to be both extensive and largely unknown today.

Vatican II and its implications led to a dramatic reduction of those pursuing religious vocations, including the vocation of the Brothers. At the same time, new opportunities and new providential circumstances led the Brothers to welcome Lasallian Partners into the Lasallian mission, including a significant number of female educators. While the number of consecrated religious men who dedicate their lives to this mission continues to decline, the number of educators who are inspired by John Baptist de La Salle, the Lasallian community, and the Lasallian charism continues to grow exponentially.

The Lasallian mission is widening and thriving in ways it never has before, and God's Providence continues to lead the way.

Over the past 50 years, Lasallian education has grown to include female students, more institutions of higher education, and a multitude of other educational and formative ministries. While the nature of the mission has remained foundationally Catholic, people of all faiths have found themselves welcome, as exemplified by those at Bethlehem University, the schools in Japan, Pakistan, and India, and other Lasallian institutions in Europe, North America, and Eurasia.

With over 1,000 schools and institutions worldwide, the Lasallian mission today encompasses some 4,000 Brothers and 90,000 Lasallian Partners who serve over 1,000,000 young people in 80 countries around the world. (Further details at www.lasallian.info). The Lasallian charism extends from summer camps for Christians and Muslims in the Sahel desert of Burkino Faso, to Kids Help Line in Australia—a free, private, confidential help line for any teen, any time, on any topic—answering 300,000 calls a year, to centers in South America that provide education and assistance to marginalized children and adolescents in need, to 64 colleges and universities extending from the Americas to the Philippines to the latest one in Ethiopia.

Those within the Lasallian educational family are part of a long, living, and loving educational movement that animates a vast amount of primary, secondary, and tertiary educational institutions, along with youth and family service agencies and other educational outreach ministries. All of them provide a human and Christian education to the young, especially the poor, in a ministry that has been entrusted to them by the Church.

Over the last three centuries, the Lasallian community of educators has transformed the lives of millions of individuals, young and old, Brothers and others. Some of these have also been recognized and celebrated by the Catholic Church. In addition to our Founder, there are 13 De La Salle Christian Brothers who have been canonized, and seven saints who were alumni or affiliated members of the Institute. In addition, 151 Brothers have been beatified, and 12 alumni and affiliated members as well. Nine Brothers have been declared venerable. In addition to these, there are countless Brothers and Lasallian Partners—both today and in the past—who have led lives of dedication and holiness and that remain largely hidden or known to only a few. As Robert Bolt wrote in his play, *A Man for All Seasons,* teachers have a small but important audience:

Sir Thomas More: *Why not be a teacher? You'd be a fine teacher; perhaps a great one.*

Richard Rich: *If I was, who would know it?*

Sir Thomas More: *You; your pupils; your friends; God. Not a bad public, that.*

Education has always been one of the most charitable of ministries, because the results of the teacher's work and example are never immediate, and they are rarely seen by them. Seeds are planted, guidance is given, quiet support is offered, choices are made, and positive relationships are fostered. Lasallian education is such an education and follows the pattern by which De La Salle viewed his own journey in life, led and "educated" by God in ways that he never fully realized until much later. God taught him by guiding so much in his life with wisdom and serenity, not forcing his inclinations and interests, moving him forward in an imperceptible way and over a long period of time so that one commitment led to another in a way that he could not foresee in the beginning. Such an approach is also a wonderful description of the deeper and best aspects of any educational endeavor.

If you have read this little book thoroughly, you will know that Saint John Baptist de La Salle was a hard-working kind of saint, praying and writing and organizing and talking and never giving up, just as a great teacher does. Even when things looked bad, or opposition was fierce, or family problems distracted him, or the cause seemed hopeless, he trusted that God would help him find a way where there didn't seem to be any way, God would provide challenges and support in equal measure, and God would, when needed, give him the kind of peace and assurance that overshadowed any possible obstacle. Such fundamental trust in another, in God's presence through another, is also at the core of a genuine teacher's convictions when encountering those who have been entrusted into his or her care. "Recognize Jesus beneath the poor rags of the children whom you have to instruct. Adore him in them."[27]

For the Lasallian educator, as for all Christian educators and indeed for simply all educators, God is near when our students are near. Following the writings and inspiration of De La Salle, Jesus Christ is the one who is discovered in the activity of teaching and in the student, and Jesus Christ is the one in whom and through whom all teaching takes place. Lasallian education has the school as its setting, the teacher as its focus, and the salvific potential of education as its inspiration. And Lasallian pedagogy is Lasallian precisely because of, not in spite of or along with, its spiritual dimensions. It is ultimately their spiritual life that motivated, shaped, and realized the pedagogy of De La Salle and his Brothers. We may express that spiritual life in different ways and via other traditions, yet their deeper currents all emerge from a common heritage and are well exemplified in the life of this unique individual.

Is it any wonder, then, that Saint John Baptist de La Salle is the teacher's saint?

EXPLORING FURTHER

www.dlsfootsteps.org – A virtual pilgrimage website that provides a much more extensive version of the story of Saint John Baptist de La Salle, with maps, videos, photos, 360-degree immersions, Google street maps, and interactive vocation-related questions for each location associated with the life and time De La Salle.

www.lasallianresources.org – A website of Lasallian resources (videos, books, pamphlets, programs, websites, etc.)

www.lasallian.info – The website for the Lasallian Region of North America (USA & Canada)

www.lasalle.org – The website for the Institute of the Brothers of the Christian Schools

www.brothersvocation.org – The Brothers' vocation website

Movie: *Saint John Baptist de La Salle, Patron Saint of Teachers*. (1968) Available on Amazon, Ignatius Press, and www.formed.org

Salm, Luke. *The Work Is Yours - The Life of Saint John Baptist de La Salle*. Romeoville, IL: Christian Brothers Publications, 1989.

Calcutt, Alfred. *De La Salle: A City Saint and the Liberation of the Poor through Education*. Oxford, England: De La Salle Publications, 1993.

Van Grieken, George. *Touching the Hearts of Students: Characteristics of Lasallian Schools*. Romeoville, IL: Christian Brothers Conference, 1999.

Aroz, Leon, Yves Poutet, and Jean Pungier. *Beginnings: De La Salle and his Brothers*. Translated by Luke Salm. Romeoville, IL: Christian Brothers Conference, 1980.

Thompson, William, ed. *Bérulle and the French School*. New York, NY: Paulist Press, 1989.

Lewis, Warren Hamilton. *The Splendid Century*. New York, NY: Quille, 1978.

References

1 Blain, Jean-Baptiste, *The Life of John Baptist de La Salle, Founder of the Brothers of the Christian Schools*, trans. Richard Arnandez (Romeoville, IL: Christian Brothers Conference, 1983), Vol. 1, Bk. 1: 60-61.

2 Lewis, Warren Hamilton, *The Splendid Century* (New York, NY: Quille, 1978), 63.

3 Lewis, Warren Hamilton, *The Splendid Century* (New York, NY: Quille, 1978), 64.

4 Thompson, William, ed., *Bérulle and the French School* (New York, NY: Paulist Press, 1989), 81.

5 Arnandez, Richard, FSC. "Primary Education in France in the Time of John Baptist De La Salle." In *So Favored by Grace: Education in the Time of John Baptist De La Salle,* 103-44. (Romeoville, IL: Lasallian Publications, 1991), 115.

6 Joseph Bergin, Church, *Society and Religious Change in France 1580-1730* (New Haven and London: Yale University Press, 2009), 308.

7 De La Salle, John Baptist, *Conduct of Christian Schools,* trans. F. de La Fontainerie and Richard Arnandez, ed. William Mann, (Landover, MA: Lasallian Publications, 1996), 161.

8 De La Salle, John Baptist, *Meditations by St. John Baptist de La Salle,* trans. Richard Arnandez, and

Augustine Loes, eds. Augustine Loes and Francis Huether, (Landover, MD: Christian Brothers Conference, 1994), 434 (Meditation 194.1).

9 Salm, Luke, *The Work Is Yours - The Life of Saint John Baptist de La Salle,* (Romeoville, IL: Christian Brothers Publications, 1989), 35.

10 Calcutt, Alfred, *De La Salle: A City Saint and the Liberation of the Poor through Education,* (Oxford, England: De La Salle Publications, 1993), 140.

11 Salm, Luke, *The Work Is Yours - The Life of Saint John Baptist de La Salle,* (Romeoville, IL: Christian Brothers Publications, 1989), 38.

12 Aroz, Leon, Yves Poutet, and Jean Pungier. *Beginnings: De La Salle and his Brothers,* trans. by Luke Salm, (Romeoville, IL: Christian Brothers Conference, 1980), 23.

13 Blain, *op. cit.,* 104-106.

14 Salm, Luke, *The Work Is Yours - The Life of Saint John Baptist de La Salle,* (Romeoville, IL: Christian Brothers Publications, 1989), 38.

15 Koch, C., Calligan, J., and Gros, J., eds., *John Baptist de La Salle: The Spirituality of Christian Education,* (Mahwah, NJ: Paulist Press, 2004), 113.

16 Salm, Luke, *The Work Is Yours - The Life of Saint John Baptist de La Salle,* (Romeoville, IL: Christian Brothers Publications, 1989), 39.

17 Calcutt, Alfred. *De La Salle: A City Saint and the Liberation of the Poor through Education,* (Oxford, England: De La Salle Publications, 1993), 171.

18 Battersby, W. J., *St. John Baptist De La Salle,* (New York: MacMillan, 1958), 65.

19 Calcutt, Alfred. *De La Salle: A City Saint and the Liberation of the Poor through Education,* (Oxford, England: De La Salle Publications, 1993), 219.

20 Salm, Luke, *The Work Is Yours - The Life of Saint John Baptist de La Salle,* (Romeoville, IL: Christian Brothers Publications, 1989), 79.

21 Among De La Salle's writings are the following: *The Conduct of Christian Schools* (In manuscript form until 1720), *Exercises of Piety for the use of the Christian Schools* (1696), *Instructions and Prayers for Holy Mass* (1698), *Teaching French Syllables* (1698), *How to Go to Confession* (1698), *Prayers for Confession and Communion* (1698), *The Rules of Christian Politeness and Civility* (1702), *Spiritual Canticles for the use of the Christian Schools* (Edited only; 1703), *The Duties of a Christian, or The Catechism of the Brothers of the Christian Schools* (1703), a large abridgment and a small abridgment of *The Duties* (1703), *Christian Public Worship* (Volume III of *The Duties;* 1703), *The Duties of a Christian* in continuous text of 3 volumes (1703), *David's Psalter and the Office of Our Lady* (Edited only; 1706).

22 Calcutt, Alfred. *De La Salle: A City Saint and the Liberation of the Poor through Education,* (Oxford, England: De La Salle Publications, 1993), 518.

23 Salm, Luke, *The Work Is Yours - The Life of Saint John Baptist de La Salle,* (Romeoville, IL: Christian Brothers Publications, 1989), 158.

24 Salm, Luke, *The Work Is Yours - The Life of Saint John Baptist de La Salle,* (Romeoville, IL: Christian Brothers Publications, 1989), 158.

25 Brothers of the Christian Schools, *The Rule of the Brothers of the Christian Schools.* (Rome, Italy: Institute of the Brothers of the Christian Schools, 2015), 11-12.

26 Blain, Jean-Baptiste, *The Life of John Baptist de La Salle, Founder of the Brothers of the Christian Schools,* trans. Richard Arnandez (Romeoville, IL: Christian Brothers Conference, 1983), 3:743.

27 De La Salle, John Baptist, *Meditations by St. John Baptist de La Salle,* trans. Richard Arnandez, and Augustine Loes, eds. Augustine Loes and Francis Huether, (Landover, MD: Christian Brothers Conference, 1994), 179 (Meditation 96.3).